श्री शिव जी की आरती

INDIA

LIVING IN AN ORNATE WORLD

JAMES WELLINGS

OUTSIDE MINAKSHI SUNDARESHVARA TEMPLE,
MADURAI, TAMIL NADU

AN ORNATE WORLD

6

India is rich in colour and ornamentation and has an incredible diversity of culture and architecture. Several major world religions originate from India, notably Buddhism and Hinduism, each producing its own style. India has embraced many cultures from abroad but somehow has always managed to keep its own identity. The Indian economy was the biggest in the world for a large part of the period between the 1st and 17th century AD. This wealth led to much extravagant architecture. However, one can see that Indians' love of colour and flair for ornamentation were reflected in all levels of society. A modest dwelling in India can give as much an indication of this as a palace.

For thousands of years, under the influence of Hinduism and Buddhism, India has produced beautiful sculpture and stone carvings. Then in the 12th century the Muslim invasion led to a new wave of ornamental styles. Both Hindu and Islamic art tend to be ornamental. Hindu art idealises nature and its sculpture aims to be three-dimensional whereas Islamic art is flat-surfaced, more abstract and symmetrical.

For similar reasons, India has an incredible richness and variety of architecture. Early Hindu and Buddhist architecture pre-dates the 12th century incursion. The Muslim invaders tended to attack Buddhist sanctuaries but were more inclined to compromise with Hindu buildings and often used their temples as mosques. Muslims found inspiration in certain elements of Hindu art, discovering similarities in its architecture, notably in domes and screens of pierced stone. The period following the invasion produced a profusion of different architectural approaches. An Indo-Muslim style prevailed in the western states whereas a more traditionally Islamic one was followed in those regions closer to the Delhi sultanate. In the 14th and 15th centuries Rajputs took advantage of the weakness of the Delhi administration by building temples and palaces in Hindu style. From the 17th century onwards architectural styles were influenced by various European invasions.

FRESCO IN HAVELI IN DUNLOD, HEKHAVATI DISTRICT

IN MOSQUE AT CHAMPANER, GUJARAT

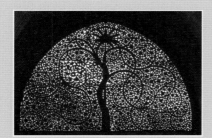

SCREEN OF PIERCED STONE, JALI AT SIDDI SALYAD'S MOSQUE, AHMEDABAD

There has been encouragement for the arts in India for thousands of years. In the 3rd century BC, Emperor Ahsoka established schools and workshops for artists and craftsmen. Later on, great patronage of the arts emanated from both royalty and merchants. The Mughals were noted for their exceptional patronage and established major workshops to train talented craftsmen in their empire. India enjoyed huge wealth during the first part of the Mughal empire, the style of living for the upper classes even surpassing that of European aristocracy. Mughal architecture included forts, palaces and tombs and reached its peak in the 17th century. The Rajputs were so amazed by what the Mughals had created in their capital, Delhi, that they also set up schools to train artists and craftsmen. Indian craftsmen had a well-organised system of guilds, very similar to that in Europe. They tended to travel widely to wherever they found work, thus spreading their skills and styles to different regions. Their patrons similarly moved about, gathering many different ideas in the process. Having selected the artistic subject, a patron would often let the craftsman develop it in his own way. It seems that Muslim and Hindu craftsmen were happy to work together.

All in all, there was a tremendous cross-fertilisation of artistic styles and ideas across India. The country was noted for the tolerance which existed between different religions and which thus absorbed creative ideas and patterns from each other. An example of this is the famous tomb of the Muslim emperor, Akbar, at Sikandra, near Agra, which was completed in 1613. Here Hindu, Christian, Islamic, Buddhist and Jain themes all blend in together. Akbar made a point of talking to all the representatives of the different religions in his empire.

7

WOMEN IN REMOTE VILLAGE IN SOUTH RAJASTHAN

COLOURS

In India one sees bright colours in so many places. Often people take the opportunity to paint them on the walls of houses, shops or temples, on doorways or other woodwork adorning dwellings, on elephants, cows' horns and even on commercial trucks. Women's saris and men's turbans display an incredible range of colours. Whole areas of cities are painted particular colours, as in Jaipur, 'The Pink City', and in Jodhpur, 'The Blue City'.

The Indian passion for colour goes back a long way. The Greek ambassador to India in about 302BC commented on their "love of adornment" and "their brightly coloured cotton garments, a brighter colour than any other." He also noted "for since they esteem beauty so highly, they do everything they can to beautify their appearance."

Colour plays a very important role in Hindu religion and culture, and some have a deep significance for Muslims. Hindus believe that the proper use of colour creates a cheerful environment. The colour of clothing is considered an indication of its quality. Different colours have different meanings for Hindus. For instance, red is of the utmost significance, indicating both sensuality and purity, and is used most frequently for marriages, births and festivals. Saffron represents fire. As fire burns impurities, it is the colour of holy men who have renounced the world. Green is for fertility, light blue for kindness and pink for love. In Islam, green is the sacred colour. Green and gold are the colours of paradise. Blue is a protective colour.

Colour can also signify location. Different villages identify themselves with varying colours and forms of dress. Men wear an incredible range of brightly-coloured turbans, each different shade indicating a special occasion or day of the week.

BUNDHI, RAJASTHAN

Folk art known as Rangoli is practised during Hindu festivals. Rangoli means, literally, a row of colours, and during such festivals decorative designs are placed in living rooms and courtyards.

8

DIGGING DITCHES IN MADHYA PRADESH

MAHESHWAR

Indians tend to have an innate sense of colour and of how to co-ordinate them. This is particularly apparent with women's saris which have a beautiful range of colours and patterns. Not only do the wearers often co-ordinate the colour of their clothes but often match those they wear with those of their houses and front doors. Also, they appear beautifully dressed, no matter what job they are doing. As an example, I have seen some attired in the most stunning colours whilst digging ditches - and managing to look very elegant whilst doing so. I am also surprised by how often I see some of the poorest people wearing lovely colours and even fine materials. It seems that in many countries, even those with hardly any possessions are determined to show the world that they can still dress beautifully. Perhaps also there is a deep seated need for colour to enable people to relieve themselves of the monotony of life or their landscape in various parts of the world.

When Ghandi was striving for Indian independence, he wanted to unify the country through cloth, choosing white because it represented purity. One can easily see that white would not have predominated naturally because Indians have such a love of colour.

India has a long tradition of producing dyes for, some say, 5000 years. This knowledge, including an understanding of which dyes will go with each other, has been past down from generation to generation. A multitude of vegetables, herbs and minerals have been used to produce a vast array of colours, with immense trouble taken to achieve the exact shade required. For example, in the Shekhavati region cows were fed on mango leaves and their urine distilled to produce an intense yellow colour.

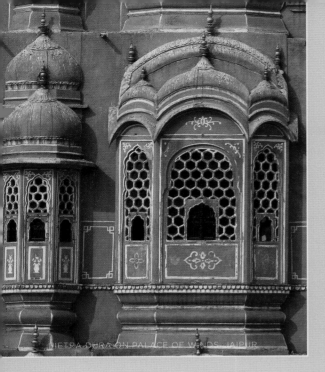
PIETRA DURA ON PALACE OF WINDS, JAIPUR

PATTERNS

India has been described as a pattern nirvana. Patterns abound on saris, turbans, jewellery, nails, feet, bodies, fabrics, doors, elephants, cows' horns, commercial trucks, bullock carts, to name but a few. Indian architecture displays a wealth of detail and is particularly noted for its repeat patterns on the exteriors and interiors of buildings. Geometrics are used to divide a building's façade into squares and rectangles, within which patterns are created. The Islamic genius for mathematics and geometry was ideally suited for this purpose.

In India, patterns on buildings are typically created by inlaying different stones and materials, a process known as pietra dura, and by stone carving. Many famous Indian buildings are noted for their red sandstone material inlaid with white marble, such as the Red Fort in Agra and the Hawa Mahal 'Palace of Winds' which is part of the Jaipur Palace.

Some buildings are of marble inlaid with other stones. A remarkable example of this is the tomb of Itimad-ud-Daulah, Agra, where the marble has been inlaid with a wide range of soft-coloured stones, in particular with a pale yellow sandstone. Perhaps the most exceptional example is the Taj Mahal, also in Agra, which is made of white marble inlaid with thin pieces of black stone. On my first visit to the Taj Mahal I felt as if I were seeing a vast ivory carving, the full impact of which was hard to take in. Thus I found it more rewarding the second time I saw it. As I walked around, I was particularly struck by the ornamentation of the multiple patterns of translucent marble inlaid with stones, some of which are semi-precious. Akbar's tomb in Sikandra is a good example of red sandstone inlaid with white marble and different coloured stones. Here you can observe the abstract patterns based on mathematics and Islamic script. You can also see intricately-carved red sandstone columns in part of the same complex of Fathpur Sikri.

ITIMAD-UD-DAULAH, AGRA

TRANSLUCENT MARBLE IN TAJ MAHAL

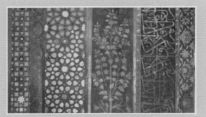
COLOURED STONE INLAY AT SIKANDRA

DOOR FROM A MANSION, TAMIL NADU

In India, there is much use of repeat pattern by painting on plaster work, utilising mirror glass, mosaics and by carving in wood. The Rajput princes particularly liked to use floral and organic patterns in their palaces. Their repeat patterns on plastered walls, their use of mirror glass and inlaid marble for decorating walls and ceilings produced remarkable results.

India is well known for its wood carving known as Jali. Elaborate woodwork is prominent in many religious buildings, particularly ancient Hindu temples with their doors, ceilings and pillars. Houses in India often have elaborately carved doorways, verandas and pillars. Wealthy merchants made a great feature of intricate wood carvings on the outside and inside of their havelis. Architectural and ornamental screens are other attractive features of Indian architecture and often follow Islamic patterns.

Another example of repeat patterns in India is hand block printing on textiles. This is done with a series of intricately carved symmetrical wooden blocks which are used to stamp the dyes on the material. Typically there will be around two or three dozen different blocks used on each material. After the patterns have been stamped onto the material it is then washed in other dyes with other colours. Some of the original dyes on this material accept the new colours and others reject them in order to produce the desired pattern. This is another example of the highly specialized knowledge about dyes which has been passed down from generation to generation for thousands of years.

The East India Company started dealing in textiles from India in the 17th century. This started a 300 year British obsession with Indian art and patterns in textiles and interior decorations. In the 19th Century many of the designs by William Morris and Arthur Sanderson were inspired by Indian patterns. William Morris took an apprenticeship with Sir Thomas Wardle who ran a textile business in Leek, Staffordshire. Wardle was researching and developing Indian silks and natural dyestuffs. Both men worked together to try to obtain the depth of colour from natural, permanent dyes by using Indian methods of dyeing. They then used these skills for hand block printing.

BALCONY IN AGRA

When visiting the old quarters of towns and cities in India one can observe the desire for ornamentation. Beautiful wooden houses, often with lovely carved verandas and pillars, are prevalent. An attractive door and doorway are clearly important. Sometimes the verandas feature elaborate metal work. Often the stonework on houses has interesting shapes which are accentuated with bright colours. Walking the streets can be a constant delight, mixing as it does all these sights together with the colourful crowds of locals while simultaneously trying to avoid cows, other animals and fast passing motor bicycles.

IN THE MARKET, AHMEDABAD

AHMEDABAD & GUJARAT

I have visited many parts of India but I have been particularly impressed with Ahmedabad and the state of Gujarat. On my first visit I made a two-week trip around the state with a local driver in a small car. It was one of my most delightful experiences, despite the fact that my driver only spoke about four words of English which just about equalled my skill in Hindi! He was always smiling and cheerful, frequently playing Hindi music as we drove around with the car windows wide open. We had a planned itinerary to various towns and historic sites, but just as pleasurable were the unexpected experiences on the way. Gujarat is one of the less-developed and least spoilt states. The lack of cars and the multitude of animals on the streets give many towns and villages a Biblical feel. One sees cows, goats, dogs, pigs, sheep and others wandering the streets, monkeys leaping about, bullocks and camels pulling carts. Cows recline in the middle of the road or the centre of some busy roundabout. In the Hindu religion, animals are worshipped like gods. One gains the impression that animals treat humans gently in response to the respect they receive themselves.

Gujarat was formerly one of the greatest textiles areas in the world, the historic centre of the creation of all manner of fabrics, particularly embroidery. It has been involved in the production of cotton for 7,000 years. Ahmedabad was a major trading centre for textiles from the 15th century; in the 19th century the city was the heart of India's industrial textile production.

I particularly enjoy visiting the old city in Ahmedabad. There are so many old wooden houses all over the area and I found the local people very friendly as I wandered around during a recent visit. I remember being greeted constantly by locals while in the old Muslim quarter on a Sunday morning. In one place where some music was being played, I was even asked by one man whether I would like to have a dance! It is quite common to see a woman or a man singing and entertaining the crowd. The market at Ahmedabad is well worth a visit and reflects the city as the historic centre of textiles. Prominent there are the stalls selling textiles and jewellery. Vast numbers of women go to the market in the afternoons, wearing their fine saris for what seems a social occasion rather than just a shopping expedition. One sees a riot of different colours.

WOOD CARVINGS ON AHMEDABAD
HAVELI

A visit to Ahmedabad's Calico Museum is an exceptional experience. Here one sees a really beautiful collection of mostly 17th and 18th century textiles of embroideries, costumes, religious paintings on cloth, woven silk, Kashmir shawls and others. I was taken around by a rather stern, matronly woman who wore a mismatch of colours - a strange phenomenon for India and especially in a museum which has such an attractive collection of textiles which all blend in together. No cameras are allowed inside and there are no pictures on sale, so sadly one comes away without any record of such a staggering visual experience.

The ancient part of Ahmedabad where artisans lived and worked is full of merchants' grand houses known as havelis which feature the most glorious carvings in their interiors and on their verandas and outside pillars. It is suggested that this decoration was carried out by the highly-skilled carvers who made the wood blocks for textile printing. This ancient area is a web of old streets, alleyways and cul de sacs, with so many beautiful old wooden houses as well as the havelis.

THE PHOTOGRAPHS

GWALIOR

India is a delight for the artist and the photographer. I love the country, for all its chaos and character in which nearly anything goes. I saw a stationary vehicle at a busy roundabout in Gwalior, with one man having something extracted from his ear by another on a bicycle. I have seen teeth being pulled out on the side of an urban road. In Varanasi I had to step aside in a small alleyway as a dead person was carried past me, covered with a thin silk sheet. After paying to go down a motorway one finds a camel and cart coming slowly down the fast lane in the opposite direction.

So many parts of India are beautiful, with all their colour and decoration. There are other areas which are grey, ramshackle and dilapidated, but out of these, beautiful visions can appear. Within a mass of people in a dark, grimy railway station, a shaft of light streams through and highlights a slim, beautiful woman in a saffron-coloured sari, carrying a basket of fruit on her head with great poise.

Local people can add so much to the scene. One sees a man sitting on something interesting and unintentionally striking a pose which accentuates his chiselled features. I think to myself that if I am not quick I shall miss the opportunity to record it, but then he remains still for ages, apparently totally unmoved by my taking a photograph! It is probably because he is in a yogic position. If one sees an interesting street scene, it is rarely long before a woman or women walk past wearing beautiful saris.

I hope the photographs in this book will give you a flavour of the atmosphere of this incredible country.

23

29

34

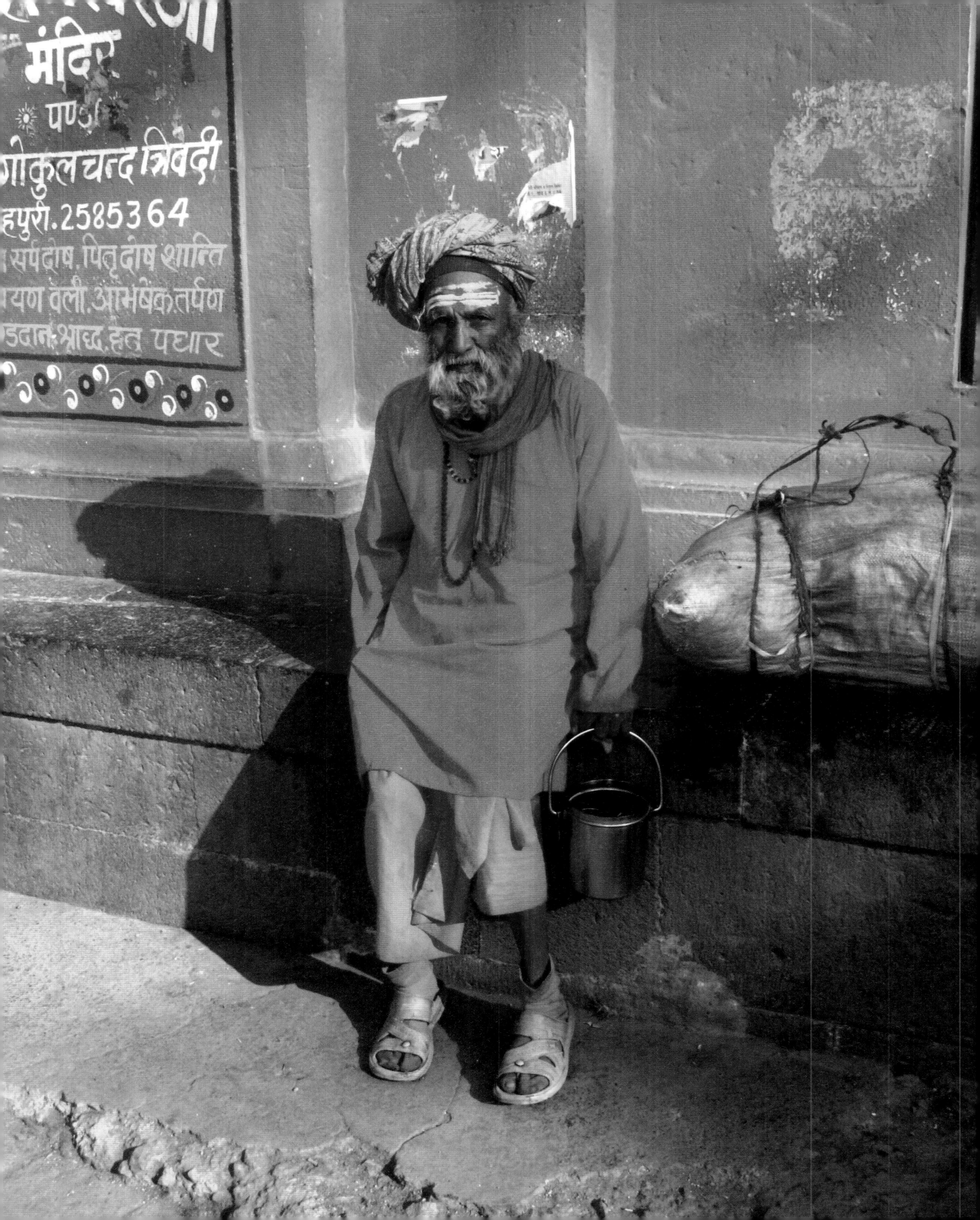
मंदिर
2585364
सर्पदोष. पितृ दोष शान्ति

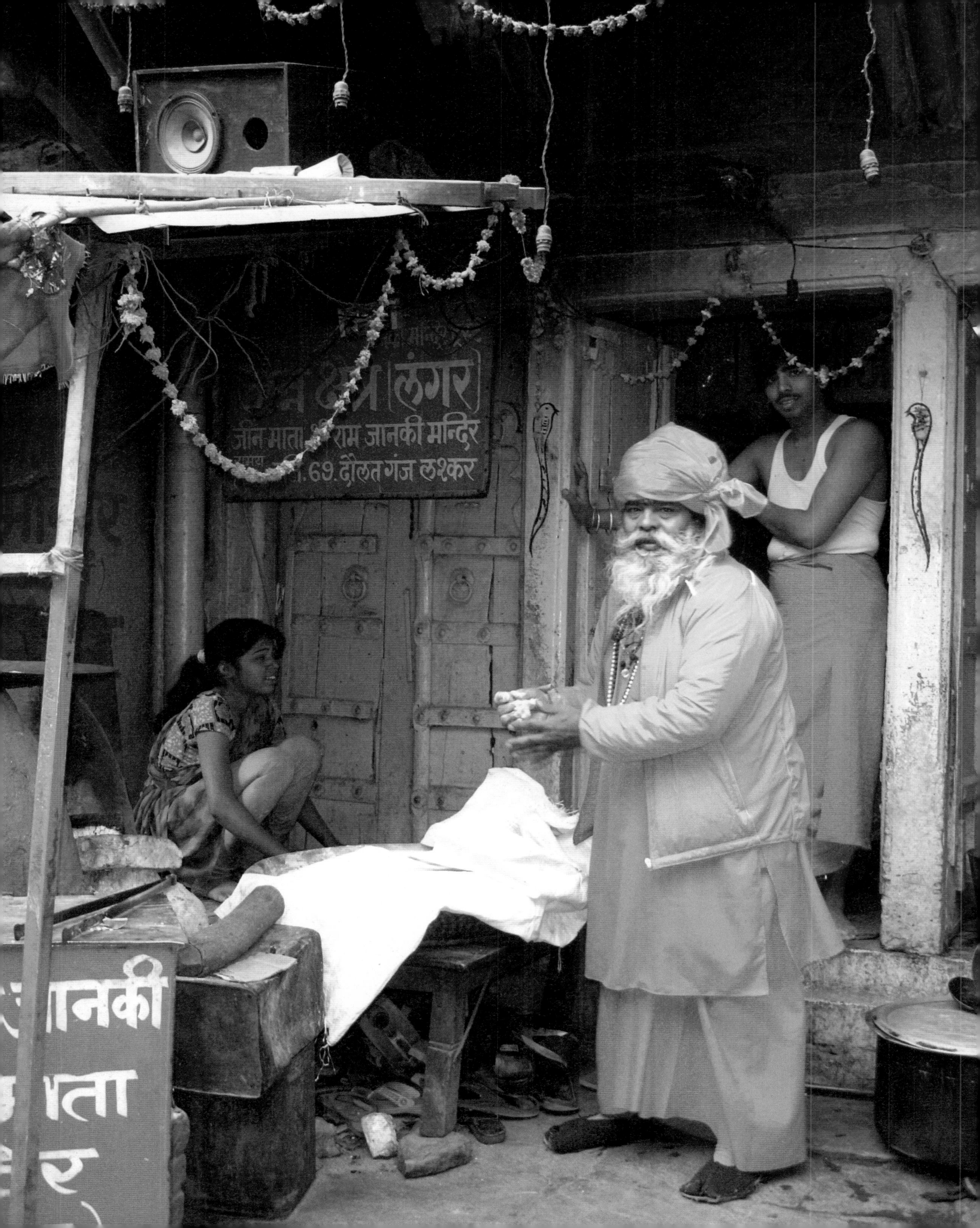
लंगर
राम जानकी मन्दिर
69. दौलत गंज लश्कर
जानकी

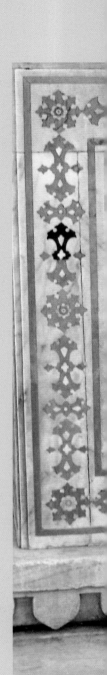

62

70

76

78

91

118

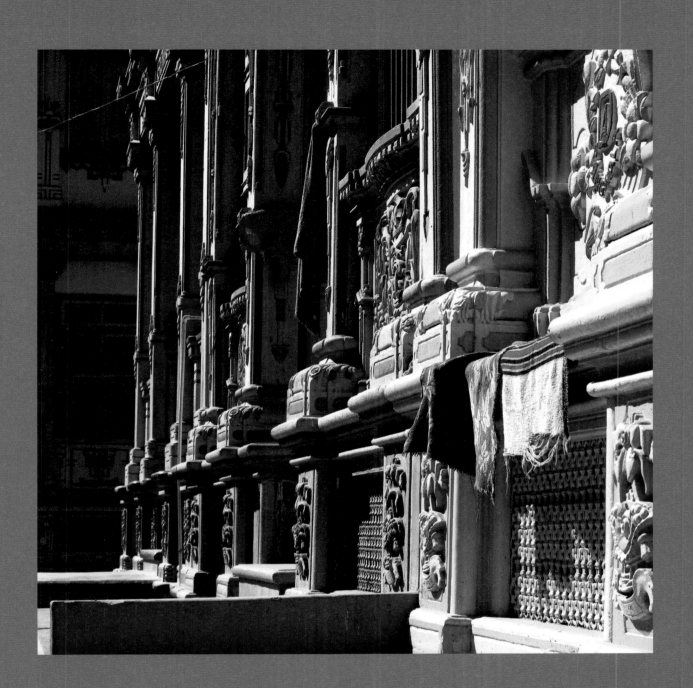

133

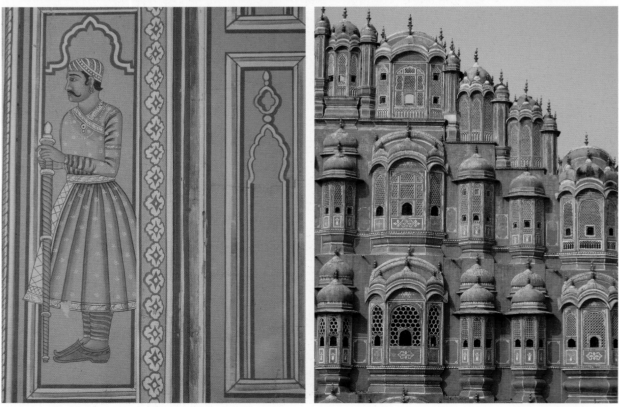

CLOCKWISE FROM TOP LEFT

INDIA
LIVING IN AN ORNATE WORLD

© JAMES WELLINGS 2015

First published in 2015 by Talisman Publishing Pte Ltd
99 Wallis Road, London, E9 5LN

ISBN 978-981-09-1354-0

All photographs and text
© JAMES WELLINGS 2015

Printed and bound in Great Britain

Designed by Charlotte Shima

Retouching by Yuki Shima

To order limited edition prints from the book and all other enquiries please email: jwellings@hotmail.com

JAMES WELLINGS

At the age of 49 James Wellings retired from stock exchange fund management and swapped his obsession with the FTSE 100 for travel and photography. He has now visited 75 countries and found nothing to rival India for colour and cultural complexity. James had an exhibition "Colours of India" in 2008 at the Piers Feetham Gallery in Fulham and after several more visits to India has gathered more photographs to add to his collection for this book.